TO: _____

FROM: _____

DATE: _____

MESSAGE: _____

_____

_____

HOMEMADE MEAL

One home-cooked meal prepared for you.
You choose the recipe!

ERRAND PASS

I'll take one thing off your to-do list today

CHORE PASS

I'll do one household chore of your choice

BUBBLE BATH

A relaxing bubble bath paired with candles, wine and music

CAMPING

One night making s'mores, even if it's in the living room

CAR WASH

MOVIE NIGHT

You choose the movie; I'll make the popcorn!

BOOZE TASTING

Your choice of beer, wine, or spirits

COUPLE'S WALK

Your choice of a morning or evening walk together

EXERCISE TOGETHER

One 30-minute session
of your exercise of choice

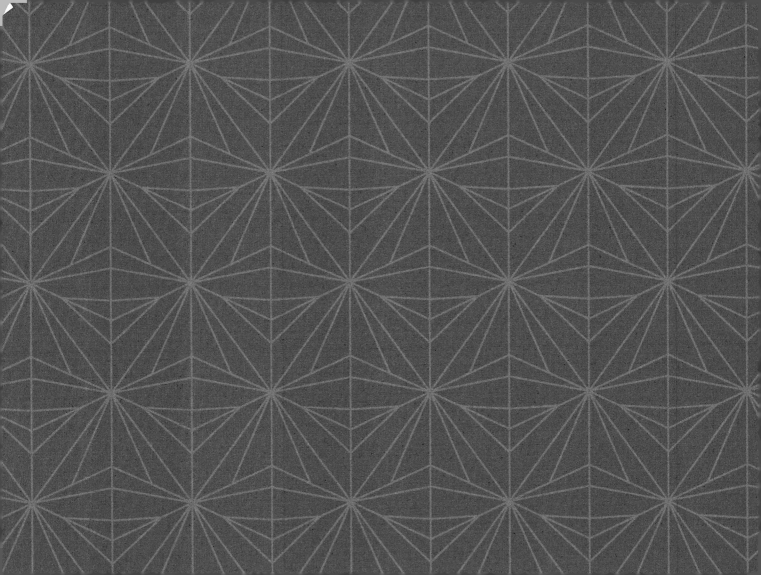

EXCLUSIVE TV RIGHTS

You control the remote tonight!

PHOTO SHOOT

One 30-minute session of taking photos together
(without complaints)

A NIGHT UNPLUGGED

One night without mobile distractions
(at least 4 hours)

WINE & CHEESE

I'll prepare everything!

WEEKEND GETAWAY

Your choice of a road trip, hotel stay, or going somewhere new!

FRIENDS' NIGHT

A friends' only night

GAME NIGHT

One night of games for two! Your choice of boardgames, puzzles, or two-player video games

DO IT OURSELVES

One afternoon spent working
on a homemade project together

COOKING CLASS

One cooking class provided for you

ROMANTIC DINNER

You choose the dinner,
I'll prepare everything

DO NOT DISTURB

A session of alone time
(maximum 3 hours)

NAP TIME

One undisturbed nap
(limited to 1 hour)

TRASH DUTY

I'll take out the trash today

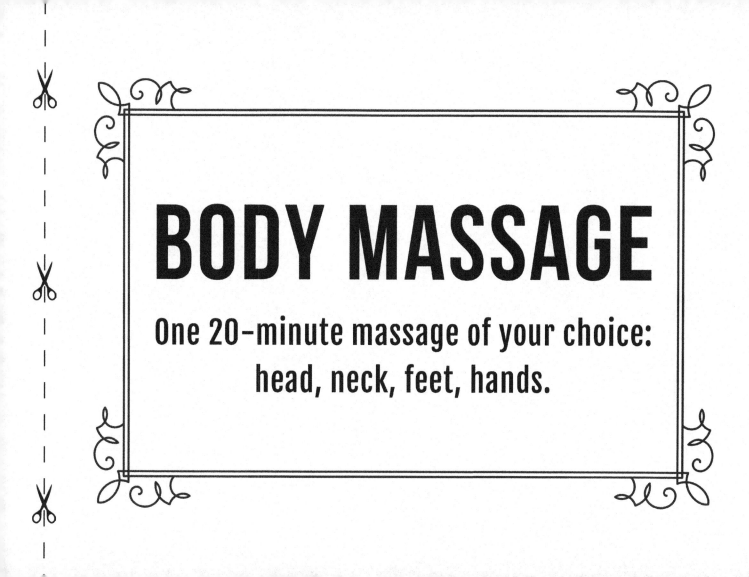

BODY MASSAGE

One 20-minute massage of your choice:
head, neck, feet, hands.

JUICY KISS

A kiss for you!

CUDDLE TIME

A 30-minute snuggle session

BACK MASSAGE

One 20-minute massage.
Your choice of deep tissue or back scratch

SHOPPING SPREE

An afternoon of shopping for two

SUNSET FOR TWO

**One evening spent admiring the sky.
I'll bring the wine!**

COOK TOGETHER

One evening spent cooking together. You choose the recipe!

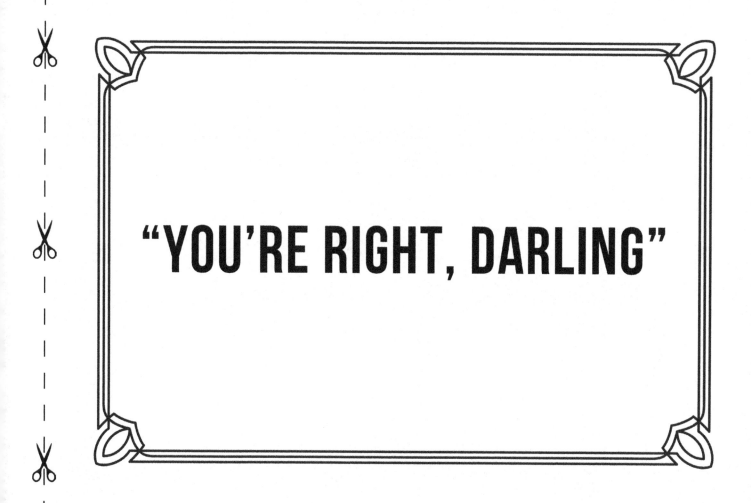

"YOU'RE RIGHT, DARLING"

STARGAZING

A night admiring the stars

COLLECT PHOTOS

One afternoon spent collecting our favorite photos to print

PICNIC DATE

An afternoon picnic with homemade food, wine, and a red checkered tablecloth

GET CRAFTY

One afternoon spent making arts & crafts

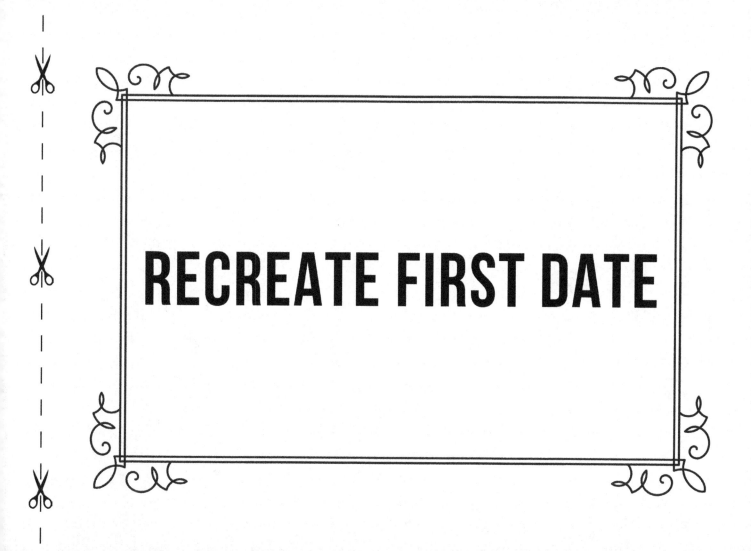

RECREATE FIRST DATE

SLOW DANCE

One slow dance to your song of choice,
even if we dance in the living room

FREE DELIVERY

I'll pick up or order in whatever you're craving!

WHERE TO EAT?

I'll take the decision off your hands this time

DESIGNATED DRIVER

That's me tonight!

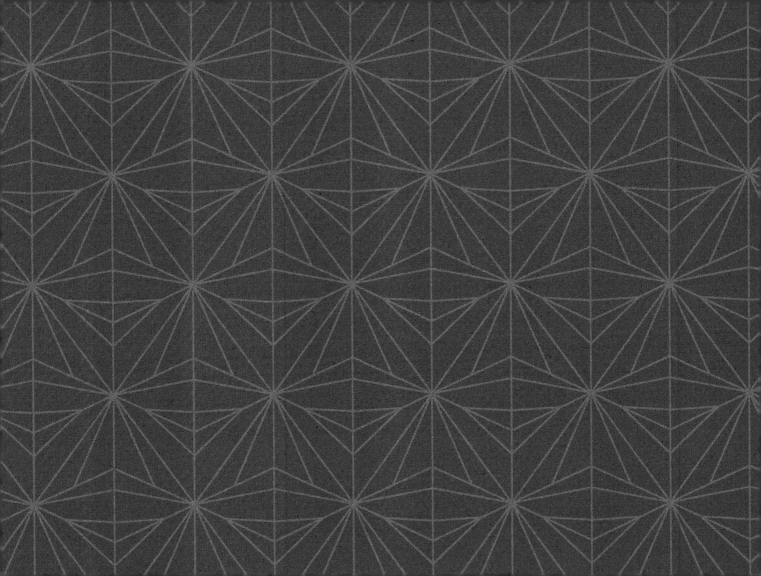

BIKE RIDE

DATE NIGHT

You get to choose!

RISE AND SHINE

One morning admiring the sunrise

DAY OFF

One lazy day spent in bed.
I can't nag you!

NEW TV SHOW

A night binge watching a new show

COUPLE'S SHOWER

One shower for two.
You control the temperature!

SWIM FOR TWO

One afternoon spent swimming together

PIZZA NIGHT

A night ordering in pizza or making our own

VISIT A PARK

**One morning, afternoon,
or evening walk in the park**

NIGHT OUT

A night spent out of the house

WILDCARD

Made in the USA
Coppell, TX
05 April 2022